The Diary of an Enchantress

Poetry, infused with themes of desire, lust, sensuality, and the magic of nature's glory.

Josephine Okujeni

CONTACT

Instagram / Facebook/ Twitter : @josephineokujeni

Email : Josephineokujenipoet@gmail.com

This book is dedicated to the lovers of nature, sunsets and to the souls forever in awe of the mysteries of the universe.

I see the temple from the brink of the mountains.

I see the temple from the brink of the mountains.

The ground which I stand, is coated with oodles of white and red rose petals.

The sound of beating drums emanating from a parallel universe, the gods respond...

If you can whisper to my ears

the sweet secrets no man or god can speak of...

And tell me a tale of fortune, where two worlds collide.

I'd bite my tongue and swallow your words like honey.

Tell me, if your heart breaks all over again,

Or if you feel utmost serenity at the presence of such a spectacle.

When all is tranquil,

and the rivers of the earth settle for clarity,

think of me yet again I pray you.

And maybe this time, our worlds truly might collide ...

Come paint my breast with lavender

Come paint my breast with lavender
clothe me in the enthralling grace of sunflowers
wrap my waist with bells of fortune
glaze my skin with raw honey
 let the sweet glow of my naked skin blend with the golden rays of the sun
while I dance to the tune of the spirits
pleasing the gods,
the Ocean bears witness,
 all that fills my heart is love,
 for it's the only euphony my soul sings.

Taste the nectar on my tongue

Taste the nectar on my tongue
as you savor me with kisses

and when the echoes of rationality intrudes this luscious reverie

I carved out for you,

never surrender to them.

Drink from my fountain.

I'll play you a song of passion, pleasure,

 and ecstasy.

We're one and the same after all

I'm bound to you

as you are to me.

I see images of you

I see images of you

lying in bed, wrapped in my crimson spread out sheets,

naked...fully naked

though fast asleep.

Worn out from the night before,

drenched with soft kisses

and slow love making

with candles ignited and

emotions exploding.

I would sit by your bed and watch you sleep

Then play a timeworn antique harp carved from many a time ago,

reeling spellbound sounds,

an elixir for the soul,

and with every note...a translucent euphony.

I will play this tune

so it seeps into your subconscious

and even in your sleep...

You will feel me.

When my hands graze the waters

When my hands graze the waters

all I crave is your touch.

I felt your kiss upon my lips as I lay afloat and bind myself to you,

dearest one.

When we touch, the earth responds.

When we kiss, I'm electrified.

Lost in the abyss of pure ecstasy,

we've circled the ties

that bind the pyramid,

only to end up at the

center of the labyrinth

where it all began.

Alas, now I see it clearly,

I breathe...

only for you.

When the foreshadowing of a new dawn unfurled itself.

When the foreshadowing of a new dawn

unfurled itself,

my heart thus began a new song.

The captivating and enchanting scent of rosemary oil encapsulated my senses,

turning the shell of numbness into pure relish.

Oh, such wonder, such bliss,

blessed with the sweet gland of nature's musk.

I'll tell it sweetly to you just how it feels, maybe in a song or perhaps a poem.

For now...

I'll adorn myself in glittering jewels,

woven from a thousand years, fit for kings and queens

of then realms

and savor what's left of its mystery

Adore me once more

Adore me once more,

infuse my fragrance amidst the lotus pot with honey,

carved by the river nymph.

I'm broken like a glass splattered across

the wooden deck

of an old, abandoned cabin by the riverbed.

The glistening rays of the moonlight.

A reflection of silver.

An order of chaos.

Dine in my chambers this new moon

and bring me a warm heart to love.

I'll fetch nectar and strawberries,

then crush fresh grapes into wine.

Essence

I've blessed my essence with the captivating scent of sandalwood,

while meditating on the Bethlehem star.

I'm enveloped with pure ecstasy,

 awash of bliss emanating from such divine celestial beings.

I'm born anew

and now, my soul dances in alignment

 with the tune of the spirit.

I witnessed the shining gem overcast

I witnessed the shining gem overcast,

farther and farther away it drifts off.

So, I beseech you now,

deliver me where the wants of my heart abide,

apprise me the richness of your tongue.

As quaint as the moon

as melodious as the hummingbird,

we've said our prayers and goodbyes

and baptized our senses with floral essence

while reminiscing to fables foretold

where the ancients weaved their braids

and bathed their skin with goat milk and honey.

Preserver of my sanity

Preserver of my sanity,

leave me spellbound

till I succumb to thy illusion,

and at the break of dawn,

I'll carry with me a wish soever longing.

The Sanctuary remained as I envisioned

The Sanctuary remained as I envisioned

Antique and timeless.

Relic aesthetics draped in crimson.

Pillars framed the scene.

A picturesque view of bright orange sunset

and chants of Maya drifting from below.

My fingers traced the rough patches of soil

plastered on the brick walls.

A part of me dared for an intrusion...

Of one who's peeves cajoled souls of men even before time.

Perhaps, not today. Not today.

As the white moon lit up the sky

As the white moon lit up the sky,

I felt the warmth of his lips bringing me back to life...

Maybe I'm crazy for the wild

Maybe I'm crazy for the wild,
All I ever could love was you.

I want to run through these pathways and dance at the hilltop.

My dearest one, meet me by the

pond.

I've painted my lips in crimson,

washed my hair with rose water,

and lie awaiting your return.

Dive into my ocean of bliss,

let it drive you insane.

Cherish it all, my darling, cherish me still.

I'm bound to you now, forever and always.

Somewhere beneath the fragrance and bosom of the trees

Somewhere beneath the fragrance and bosom of the trees,

lies a secret...

mystifying, feminine and gentle at heart.

I surrendered to the wonders of such a specter.

The glory of the divine.

Written all over the ambiance of nature's beauty.

A whisper...or a song?

The language of the spirit of the waters.

A perfect blend with lusters of its sphere.

One can only relish.

When I feel the rays of the sun kiss my cheeks

When I feel the rays of the sun kiss my cheeks,

I think of you.

Don't hold back.

Let me in,

draw near, I pray you.

Petals lay masking the ground below us,

 hands circling around the bare bosom.

In the rush of frenzy,

we are one.

I like my mornings dancing to Apollo's lyre

I like my mornings dancing to Apollo's lyre...

as the scent of a champagne toast candle drifts into the air.

I embark on a quest to seek the fruit of my essence.

I embark on a quest to seek the fruit of my essence.

Toes in sand, planted upon the face of the earth, sending chills down my spine,

It is now or never.

Farther and farther, I go

till the ground below me gives way.

Such grace the ocean before me bears...

Oh, the feeling of isolation within the great and vast sphere

of the underworld.

Deeper and deeper, surging through the depths of this strange

but tranquil realm.

My body naturally moves to its rhythm.

Swaying, gliding with every flow, wave, and rush...

I am free, free at last.

Lost at sea and found within.

Only for this blessed period.

For it washes away the filth and dismay

that weighs upon my tender heart from many a time ago.

Rising from the depths, gliding my way through the tide...I feel reborn.

Touch me with your words

Touch me with your words.

Unravel me if you dare.

I'm lying open like a flower,

to bloom only for you, my dear.

The sensual aroma of coffee lingers in bed

The sensual aroma of coffee lingers in bed…

Skin barely covered in silk night dress.

Poetry at hand,

melody at heart.

The euphony of serenity blends with tranquility,

Soon, my soul would sing along.

In bed, I lay

the stars aligned above, starry clouds floating the ceiling.

A whisper of a new day,

with sunlight bleeding in through crimson curtains.

Amusement of the day before... I think of you sometimes.

Reminiscing...

the ambiance of luxury mixed with majestic hues;

nature embodied that warm afternoon on the shores of Palos Verdes.

Succumbing to the nature of the now

Succumbing to the nature of the now.

Ice latte in one hand. A dream in the other.

I think of you sometimes... You seep through my mind

like a misting fog making its way through

the crack of a closed door.

When I read a sultry passion-soaked line in a novel or poem,

I see your face again.

I can almost taste you again.

The raw passion reignited.

Triggered by luring and seductive words you enchant me with…

Like your dreams of me in Paris.

It's like I feel you all over again,

Your eyes, resting on mine.

How you wrap your

hands around me... drawing close with every breath

I sink in deeper into

your embrace...

...You're the only one I think about when I read an erotic book, filled with lewd escapades.

A burst of frenzy.

Reveling...

Yes, I think of you sometimes... and wonder if you

think of me too.

A tale of lost cities and queendoms,

A tale of lost cities and queendoms

sheltered by the seven wonders of the world.

I bind this truth to thee

and pray your promise, you

keep.

I sang a melody of taboos at nightfall,

a song from the heart,

a language known only to the keepers of

all that is.

We kissed the same lips whilst bleeding love ensued,

yet you act surprised, like my soul never

yearned for you,

 like my heart does not beat only for you.

Watch me mesmerize you with my slow, mysterious prances.

I kneel before you, not to pray

but to serve,

to serve your very hunger, to quench your thirst,

to fulfill your deepest desires.

After all,

 I am that which is realized at the climax of all yearnings.

Closed my heart to yet another tale of passion

Closed my heart to yet another tale of passion.

Caught a whiff of desire now I've lost all marbles.

A mystic trance leading to a clandestine liaison with the enchanter.

A dreamlike stance sunken in sweet reverie

A dreamlike stance sunken in sweet reverie,

a floral fragrance of plum blossom to arouse...

arouse the senses ...arouse the muses.

Listen closely, and you just might hear the stringed instrument...

playing an endless melody

the ancient ones would sing along,

still your mind and you just might

feel the heat emanating from the hot sand of the Sahara Desert

or catch a whiff of the subtle scent of myrrh and frankincense

drifting from the incense markets.

Surrendering to the present.

Surrendering to the present

A magical feeling of emancipation

from the strongholds of a worrisome heart,

of that which is unseen.

Basking in the radiance of time

 The glory of the now.

The flame in me is rekindled,

and it warms my heart like a lover's touch.

I dance freely in the gardens of wishes

and wash my hands in the

stream of desire,

while love remains my

only companion.

This present time is all I have and know.

Oh,

 how romantic it all feels...

So wealthy I have become,

since time became my lover.

The gift of the present, the glory of the 'now'.

I would remember you

I would remember you

through the changing fortunes of time.

My soul would forever dance to the tune of your essence.

I'm intoxicated by your aura.

Tears well up in my eyes when you see through my heart.

This is but poetry to the soul.

I'm enchanted by you.

Such serenity and seduction of the mind.

Such glory, such power.

I lay still in this sacred place

we found in solitude and pray to thee I'm never alone.

Beyond the veils of normalcy

Beyond the veils of normalcy,

there's a hint of the extraordinaire,

the fruit of magnificence.

Within the spinning hole of the illusory whirlwind

lies the base for restoration.

You close your eyes to see the true nature of life realities.

I felt the presence of the ones before me.

The divine beings, basking in the glory, emanating from all.

My heart draws them near.

Their words I hold dear,

this safe space I cherish till eternity...

He says it is a part of me now.

'Just do,' he tells me...

For I've thought, dreamt, and analyzed it all ....

Now is the time to just be.

Words like honey

Words like honey,

such sweet savor to my ears,

never a tame moment.

I could drown in your embrace.

Lay next to me,

watch the stars as they sparkle,

surrounding us with such delight.

I never want to leave.

I blush at your kisses.

I am enchanted

by you.

You seem to be telling me it's time to

go

but time better wait this one out,

 for this…

this is my true escape.

We've scaled the highs and lows,

We've scaled the highs and lows,

traveling through tides of chaos.

Losing knots of confusion,

only to find Peebles grounded on our path,

leading us to this sacred sanctuary, we now lay in solitude.

Orchids in the garden

Orchids in the garden

nor lambent skies

do not compare to the beauty I see in your eyes.

All that has life within, beckons at your gaze... lost in awe.

Such glory, such warm delight. My sweet, sweet escape.

I wept for you under the mystical tree

I wept for you under the mystical tree

Iroko,

right by the flames emanating from these ashes of our past.

There I wept, night after night.

Such serenity and seduction of the mind

Such serenity and seduction of the mind.

Such power, such glory thy possess.

I see it all in you.

The beauty of the divine,

the mystery of the universe.

You only need do what you can.

Heed to thy call, day and night.

Listen to the euphony of the spirit,

avoid the waywardness of man

and remain deviant till the very end.

Lie in solitude,

for there, the soul is strong.

You and I are very much alike.

You, my muse, and I, your musing.

A twinkle in his eyes,

A twinkle in his eyes,

A swing in his step,

this risqué boy from the islands,

comes only to woo and cajole.

I know what he wants.

I know what he desires.

The spell lingering

between my thighs.

With a dainty charm like that,

 How can a girl think straight?

Players caper,

now playboy has come to play.

He lures me till I lose myself,

silly with words

and never serious...

Like a gun,

he shot a bullet with his

tongue,

hitting all the right places.

Lips that arouse,

leaving me bleeding pure lust.

The call to ripen is woven in deep secrets

The call to ripen is woven in deep secrets,

secrets that tear apart the walls of the fainted heart.

She loved the visions,

she danced to every tune

but neglected the concealed tidings

beneath such a specter.

For it wasn't one milked with honey.

It was one born with sweat, pain, and tears.

This is no easy ride,

you see,

only ultimate perseverance begets such mastery.

The art of living and being

which truly transforms men into gods.

It is but the absolute forbearance of sanity.

I'm not the ' long walks along the beach' type.

I just want to sit in front of the ocean and get lost in it's peaceful embrace.

When the sun rays invade our clandestine sanctuary

When the sun rays invade our clandestine sanctuary

through window panes,

I smile...

reminiscent of the night before,

 replaying the tape in my mind

over and over.

It draws in nature's delight.

A peak, a spectacle of eroticism

Sweat glistening skin wrapped in silk sheets,

 legs intertwined.

A fragrance of desire

bounded in the aftermath of lustful escapades.

When you catch a whiff of sandalwood fragrance

When you catch a whiff of sandalwood fragrance

drifting from my breast...

succumb

as it draws you near

so you drink in all of my glory, my love.

Ancient one

Ancient one,

your means faster than the shooting star,

my silk garments have engulfed the wetness of this stream.

The power of such magnitude.

We are nothing alike, you say,

By dawn, I'll go my way.

I'll wash my feet with water squeezed from petals of fresh roses

and grease my lips with

a squash of succulent berries.

Another lie of lust foretold,

in misery sham and dismay.

Cast me into the abyss of insanity,

 after all, time is but an illusion and I've longed for you

even before her very beginnings.

I'm bounded to the rune of tales by moonlight

I'm bounded to the rune of tales by moonlight,

the unsung hymns of our humble beginnings,

coated with lust, love, betrayal,

and

I've severed ties with my conniving adversary.

Deliver me into thy bosom of illusion once more,

where gardens bloom in all four seasons and colors of lust dance in tantalizing hues,

for love can be fatal when wishes would conspire with desire.

I'll carry you in my heart for days on end

I'll carry you in my heart for days on end,

through endless fortunes of time

and wish for you a heartbreak

Only my kiss can heal.

I sealed my fate in dreams of lust, love and betrayal

I sealed my fate in dreams of lust, love and betrayal.

Shameless affection buttered by whimsical notions.

Forsake me not into the arms of desire,

lest I surrender to its delirium.

I'll trade my wishes for nectar

and heal my wounds with its sweetness.

I want to drink red wine on a porch in Italy

I want to drink red wine on a porch in Italy,

overlooking the canal

while a pianist plays a solemn tune.

Opposite me is my lover, seated.

His eyes piercing into mine,

hints of lights above

reflected

in his gaze

as his eyes rest upon mine,

no words spoken.

Still,

We fully seem to understand the silence between us.

It rarely rains in California

It rarely rains in California,

So, I lay in bed,

accompanied by the sound of falling rain,

 stemming from a gadget of some sort,

and for a moment,

I forget where I am.

All I know is that

it is raining...

and my senses are reawakening...

Blow me away with warm kisses

Blow me away with warm kisses,

like candle flames

extinguished by a puff of air

escaping the lips of a

celebrant soul.

All I ever desire

All I ever desire

is a striking and earth-shattering liaison, it banishes the norm.

Catlike is my walk, snakelike is my move

Catlike is my walk, snakelike is my move,

drown in my aura

then touch me with your words.

Though I feel your presence here and now...

I'm lost in the euphony of the ancient.

Join me in this reverie and together,

we bound our souls to the wildness of pure ecstasy.

I seem to have fallen in love with love

I seem to have fallen in love with love.

It soaks through my mind like a moist sponge,

 dripping rose-scented lather,

and I feel it all around me.

Like, when I stare at a tree and watch as the leaves flutter softly,

slowly dancing to the soft breeze.

Or

when long skimpy grasses,

sway from side to side,

waltzing to the tune of the wind.

A mystical affair.

... When water from a fountain,

slowing drips into an open pool of water

and you see the striking apparition of the warm sun

reflecting across the surface of the waters.

That must be the feeling of love,

when everything around you is painted in beauty,

when your senses are so awakened,

you feel your heart is as open as the sky, to feel love.

To love...to give love.

Do it with love, my darling

Do it with love, my darling,

do it for me.

How subtle is the view from up here?

How wonderfully crafted is it?

I see the hues of love,

a colorful harmony,

the river flowing through garden pathways,

the cries of children playing in the field,

the masters of the temple...

The mothers, the fathers and all that breathes... and now, you see me

oh, how you see me,

and you see it all, don't you?

you hear the music

you hearken to thy call

you know the song of thy heart,

you know how my soul yearns for you,

how it yearns to touch you,

to feel your pain,

to dry your eyes,

to hold you

to kiss you...to warm the depths of your heart.

You hear my call, knowing truly,

 you are my very soul's flame.

I have come to find myself

I have come to find myself

seated on this raft,

floating swiftly and gliding slowly

on the vast body of water,

the subtle waves of the ocean softly rocking me gently...

I arise

blessing my sight with the captivating view and scenery.

A whole new world,

from the distance, up ahead,

I see it...

It is huge, magnificent, and unreal.

The largest, breathtaking Ziggurat my eyes has ever been blessed to rest upon,

we go forth,

I and the ones before me, slowly... gently

and with time, we are fully present in this tabernacle.

...I feel its darkness welcome me.

I feel the coolness of nothingness embrace me, humbling me

and within seconds, the aura of my soul responds.

My spirit essence radiates,

such radiance...

a sight to behold.

Thus, it begins

Thus, it begins

I, too, welcome the darkness,

the darkness of nothingness.

Pure, undiluted tranquility...

In time, I am basking in the light.

My soul, spirit, and body are transformed.

The old sheds, the new...comes to be.

I bask in this glory.

I've longed for this gift.

And when I embark into the threshold

and plant myself at the base,

the energy from the center of the earth

aligns with my spirit

leaving me fully redeemed.

The picture of birds flying, embellish the sky.

The picture of birds flying, embellish the sky.

Ships sailing to and fro,

feet dug deep in the sand.

I pray only to get lost in this

moment.

Surrender to nothing

but the serenity of such scenery.

He asked, "What's on your mind?"

He asked, "What's on your mind?"

I responded, "I want to write..." about how my heart skips a beat

when you rest your gaze upon my face

or lie next to me on rumpled red sheets.

When we spend every waking minute together,

trivializing all that is.

When we sit under a tree,

listening to the subtle sounds of stringed instruments from many a time ago.

When we dance hand in hand to a song that can only be heard in our hearts...

Leaving others to ponder.

I want to write about how you make me feel

I want to write about how you make me feel.

A feeling of warmth in such a cold lonely world.

You caress my intuition and replace uncertainty with absolute bliss

and as the stars bling to hold our gaze...

I feel your touch engulf my senses like a flame.

Look elsewhere, my love

Look elsewhere, my love

Look to the stars

Look to the skies

Look to the trees

Look to the waters if you may

And find me in all you see,

I pray you.

A dreamlike scenery

A dreamlike scenery

bright orange sunset

pouring itself onto the surface of the ocean waves.

 The sailors abound.

I'm in awe of such a majestic spectacle.

Ah! the beauty of sunsets.

I danced to the rhythm of the day

I danced to the rhythm of the day.

The wind chased me to the trees,

wind blowing fiercely, strands of hair flying all over my face,

tears streaming down my cheeks.

The wind intense and unapologetic,

shivers at noon,

 the curse of march afternoons.

Still, I danced to the rhythm of the day.

Shrimp and cocktails with the wise one,

the scene of fancy sailboats grazing still waters,

writing poetry with a rush,

wishing I had but a vessel of my own.

I danced to the rhythm of the day.

He said, never have expectations, just go with the flow of life,

that makes me a happy man

as failed expectations lead to disappointments.

A contended, lonely life well lived,

and so, I danced to the rhythm of the day.

I pick up a pen to write

I pick up a pen to write

my mind's blank and I'm lost for words.

I try not to stare in your direction,

hair as sleek as milk

and a body frame that confuses the mind.

Do you even know how beautiful you are?

I dream of an evening in Rome with you.

Me, in a silk nightdress, drinking Champagne from a flute glass

while Beethoven plays in the distance

and you, sitting on the bed,

staring out through ceiling to floor window panes,

lost in the ray of the bright orange sunset.

I imagine what making love to you would be like.

How you'd feel when I gasped your name softly as we devour each other,

moving to the rhythm of our bodies, colliding in pure eroticism.

The only fragrance our clandestine bond share.

I want to taste those lips

I want to taste those lips

and feel the budging beast

pressed hard against my

grinding hips,

running my hands

through your chest,

we sync in

motion...

Till we surrender

exhaustively...

"Come as you are" he said

"Come as you are" he said,

my feet pressed deep

against the flowing breast of the earth.

I hear your voice, my love,

 your warnings to stay

connected to all that abounds.

The chambers you built me, welcomed me with the sweet scent of floral blossoms.

I watch as you play your favorite tune,

 fingering your lyre, honoring our vows.

I am to devote my spirit and soul to the bond we share,

lay my desires beneath the carvings of the oracle

and give my all to you.

This world of bliss, absolute bliss,

music, dance, and the captivating beauty of nature,

 is truly all I know.

Grand assurance

Grand assurance.

A perpetual union of souls.

Glorify this path and thrust forth built-up desires

into the castle of devotion,

planted in the middle of the lake.

There I lay my precious jewels,

engraved in them are stories from a parallel universe,

and unsung hymns of love lost from thousands of years.

The glare of obscure celestial beings' beckons at me

The glare of obscure celestial beings' beckons at me,

inflaming my subconscious,

arousing my intuition.

I want to get lost in this feeling and obsess over its alchemy.

I feel the power uproot my feet from the stronghold of gravity,

higher and higher I go

into the wind and mist of the clouds.

The taintless air, my companion.

A magnificent spectacle of the world below me,

 one I called home for centuries.

Soaring swiftly,

I'm emancipated, soaring gracefully,

I'm boundless,

towering above the clouds...

I'm liberated,

and as I look down on the vast realm of the earth...

I know now, I'm free to choose wherever I please and call it home.

I could set my gaze upon such gallant scenery for hours and not miss a thing.

As the chilling grip of the waters overpower my senses,

bringing me to my knees...

I watch as wave after wave collapses unto itself.

A mystical rhythm.

I hear the ocean roar and the wind blowing softly in alliance with the ferocity of her essence.

Such spectacle to behold

Such spectacle to behold,

such poetry to the soul...

and halfway where the ocean meets the sky,

I think to myself,

Whatever could be more fascinating than this?

The orange sunset pours herself into the ocean,

and the waves dance in unison

to her amusement.

Escape into thy world of sensuality

Escape into thy world of sensuality,

dance, and lovemaking.

I dance the dance of enticement

only to arouse

and to please.

Watch closely the rhythm of my hips,

let your mind swim boundlessly

to the fluidity of my very essence.

Like fingers tracing lace on brassiere

and hands caressing belly down to waist, then thighs...

allow the tune of the ancients, draw you in.

After all, it is a red moon tonight,

and the waves of ecstasy

stay unleashed.

I want you to feel every inch of me with no hands

I want you to feel every inch of me with no hands.

Breathe me in and hold.

Let me infiltrate your every cell.

I'm all the drug you need, my love.

Like a pill enraptured with portions

Sink me in.

Let go.

Surrender.

The sound of crackling fire

The sound of crackling fire

accompanied by solemn piano playing...

Poetry, the theme of the day.

Candle wax of strawberry cake

melts into an aromatic pudding.

The joys of solitude.

A luxury for the soul.

A dream of a lifetime.

When the soul hearkens, and all is still...

I feel your presence all around,

when the ego is at bay,

I hear your song drifting with the wind, senses exalted,

memories ignited.

A collision of destinies.

I carry a piece of you wherever I go,

and know that now and always,

you remain my soul's true desire.

Mist covered mountains circling the horizon

Mist covered mountains circling the horizon.

Fiercer, the waves become...

Closer to my seating, it gets,

as the sun recedes its shine,

sending me further and further

into the land of men,

leaving me astounded

as can be.

I try not to stay in bed long after the break of dawn

I try not to stay in bed long after the break of dawn.

For when I do,

thoughts of you begin to slip

through my mind.

Like the venom of a deadly snake,

slowing making its way through

the veins of its wounded prey...

With time, it slips through my heart then into my brain,

till I become consumed by the

infective thoughts of you.

So, when I begin to succumb to the poisonous thoughts

of all that makes me desire you...

I snap out of it. Spurt right up

and begin dancing to the sound of beating drums,

drowning out all aching thoughts of you.

Like a fool

Like a fool,

I held on to the glare of

ambition,

only to shatter woven promises

and lose my sanity at its demise.

Might I be silly to succumb to such

gullible notions?

Like the blind following the blind,

I fell victim to sugary coated lies, banishing the divinity bestowed.

I fell color blind to the rays of passion and sensuality.

The sweetness of nature's promise.

Such woos of men,

though enticing, are but a snare to the mind and spirit.

So, I bow to withdrawal and break the strongholds of this vicious bond.

The peace derived from dwelling in the presence of nature

The peace derived from dwelling in the presence of nature...

like medicine mixed with magical words or incantations,

they bring restoration and solace to the depth of one's heart.

I stay in awe of the uncertainty

I stay in awe of the uncertainty.

The pleasantries of new beginnings.

I'm a model in disguise for chaos and seduction.

For it is a fairy's world after all.

And all that's lost...isn't really lost.

Only with travesty,

would thy snares be broken.

Your presence feels like

Your presence feels like...

a healing balm to a wounded heart

a melodious tune to a silent trail

a spark in motion

a feeling of bliss derived from a lover's promise

a soothing warmth

a rekindled dream

a fairy's wishful desire

a beautiful dream unraveling...

The scent of fresh roses after a warm bath lingers

The scent of fresh roses after a warm bath lingers,

damp hair dripping with rosemary oil,

wrapped in crimson bathrobe,

adventures of the day unknown.

I sit in this stillness and listen.

I could sit here for hours,

just listening...

Such feelings transcribed into words,

 pictures of the subconscious

framed for my musings.

I love this feeling.

I know this feeling.

Watching candle wax melt into liquid,

I embrace this feeling.

Here and now is all that matters,

here and now is all I know.

Music, the gift and time, an illusion.

This present gift of the ' now'...

I'll cherish it for a lifetime.

With hopes that this smell of roses lingers on...

accompanying me through the changing fortunes of time.

What bliss? What notion?

What bliss? What notion?

The price is never what it seems.

With or without,

We are forever intertwined.

Our soul's essence knows no bound.

The timeless journey would always...

always bring us back to the very beginning,

the genesis of it all,

the very source, the very reason.

This is the key to all of life's mysteries.

The ultimate balm to every bruise.

Acceptance fuels desire, desire humbles the mind

and passion which avails existence, prevails.

My heart is as open as the vast blue sky

My heart is as open as the vast blue sky,

though raving notions seeps through the turmoil

that ensnares my psyche.

Still,

in you, I found the flair.

So, I'd soar like an eagle

and paint my wishes across the clouds itself.

So, all would see,

all would feel

and all would savor...

Nothing stays forsaken for too long.

Tell me another tale

Tell me another tale,

make it simple,

tragic,

heart-wrenching.

Let it soak my mind like a plague,

where lovers drown ,

and no one laughs last.

For like they say,

happy endings are stories,

left unfinished.

Mother Nature is drawing me closer to her bed

Mother Nature is drawing me closer to her bed.

I long to be the beauty I see in her.

I long to fly above the clouds with a heart as light as an angel's halo.

I long to bring forth the golden light from within

and let it glide all over me

like the glistening tip of a magic wand,

glazing my skin so softly, with a hint of the supernatural.

Life springs forth, from beneath the roots of the earth.

Life springs forth, from beneath the roots of the earth.

So vibrant,

strong and powerful.

Oh! The beauty of nature. The very beginning,

the rebirth.

To feel renewed.

To feel reborn...

"Life's too short," they say.

"Life's too short," they say

So, live every moment like it's your last.

Fuel your hearts with the flames of desire,

the passion that could either soothe or destroy.

For what good is living if no risks are taken.

Inebriation.

I sometimes prefer when I succumb to inebriation,

for only then will the folly in me come out to play.

Breaking forth barriers and doing the most,

my sober self would frown upon.

Awoken at the break of dawn

Awoken at the break of dawn,

my soul hungers for a spell.

An enchantment,

captivating,

sending me into abysmal reverie.

Sinking deep into the sultry charms of euphoria.

I lose myself.

It's 6AM, and I open my fridge to quench my thirst.

My eyes rest upon the chilled water beckoning at me.

But all my heart yearns for is the ravishing wine

 resting upon my leftovers.

"It's too early for that" I warn myself...

Then, I remember time is but an illusion.

And most of all,

somewhere on the shores of the river Niger,

is sundown.

With satisfaction, I bless my taste buds with the richness of sweet wine

 and lose myself once more.

Lay me down beneath the wet surface of the earth

Lay me down beneath the wet surface of the earth,

let my skin be awakened by the chilling grip of Mother Earth.

For her touch is my only ingredient to eternal

liberty...

Wordless music takes me to another dimension

Wordless music takes me to another dimension.

Visions of dance on a hilltop.

To get lost in a world of the unknown.

A clandestine liaison with the enchanter…

the bearer of music and keeper of the muses.

A night of a thousand tales.

I want to borrow your time for a little while

and kiss your lips all through the moonless night.

Like lotus flower caressing bare skin,

 rapt in grave ecstasy.

An abomination for the saints.

Poison my dreams with visions of you

Poison my dreams with visions of you.

Breaking every rule known to sanity.

The curse of a lifetime.

Raptured only in blissful delusions.

Let me swim and glide through the waters of uncertainty,

In its form, I'll find salvation.

Immense passion

Immense passion,

is the feeling I evoke when I lay my eyes upon you.

You call it desire, I call it inclination.

Carnality fuels like a storm.

 Growing...

Ascending...

Till suddenly,

it erupts...

If hallucinations were real life

If hallucinations were real life,

It would truly be a movie.

 Pictures of the mind,

 triggered into the

frame of reality.

Sweet, sour, bitter...

All intertwined, for the amusement of the unseen.

You hear her footsteps slowly approaching

You hear her footsteps slowly approaching,

wooden footwear tapping hard against solid rock.

Yet, grounded to the earth, she remains.

You catch a whiff of her scent before you lay eyes on her.

The sweet aroma of sandalwood,

with a touch of ylang ylang,

exploiting and possessing your senses.

Still...

Pay attention when she looks you in the eye,

like a seed concealed within the luscious ball of juice,

A story woven in pleasure, passion, and pain lies hidden.

If the universe

if bliss

if consciousness

if nature

if beauty

if the divine

if truth

were in human form.

Trust, it wouldn't be too far away.

As I swam the waters of my villa

As I swam the waters of my villa,

my gaze came to rest upon this poor creature...

A bee.

No sense of survival in such an aquatic territory

but with might, it preserved.

Struggling to scale through the merciless marine world.

I felt pity ...

This poor creature,

the enricher of honey and nectar for the gods.

I took into my hands a little scale of branch

and helped this dying creature glide swiftly.

Call it bee intuition,

 it gripped the little branch with its tiny hands and feet,

and together,

we scaled the waters till we reached the edge,

 with the bee, still gripping the branch.

I lifted it out of the water...

Laying on dry grounds.

It becomes still.

Motionless.

No more kicking its tiny hands and feet.

This poor creature fought to stay alive

and graze the nectar of another sunflower's floret.

Sadly...

it stood no chance,

and still, it remained.

Till the convention of ants came forth

and made away with it.

Oh! The fragility of life itself.

My poor, poor bee friend.

She wept tears that flowed all the way down to her bended knees

She wept tears that flowed all the way down
 to her bended knees,

and with each droplet,

a resounding spark of lightning,

even the priestess and gods could not fathom.

And slowly but surely,

a stream that would never run dry would be born.

Born to spring forth new life, revival and

eternal peace

that would forever be unshaken.

I want to walk down this path a thousand times,

till the trees dance solely to the rhythm of my heart,

and every leaf knows my name.

To be continued...

I found myself in a world I truly belong…

About the author

Josephine Okujeni is a Nigerian actress, musician and dancer based in Los Angeles, California.

Mostly known for her afro fusion sounds and belly dance. She's starred in numerous tv/film, commercials and made cameos on music video pieces.

She lives a quiet, solitary life and remains deviant to her passion of writing poetry, making music and dancing .

She also enjoys spending time in gardens, beaches and lakes. Besides writing poetry, She loves to play the harp.

'The diary of an Enchantress', which is her first book, is a collection of poems centered on the themes of passion, lust and the magic of nature's glory.

She's currently working on her second book, a tale with nubs of a mystical adventure and immense passion from a recherché affair.

JOIN JOSEPHINE OKUJENI ON THE FOLLOWING:

INSTAGRAM: https://www.instagram.com/thediaryofanenchantress/ FACEBOOK:

https://www.facebook.com/jokujeni TWITTER:

https://mobile.twitter.com/josephineokujen YOUTUBE :

https://youtube.com/c/JosephineOkujeni

Printed in Great Britain
by Amazon

82446616R00058